In 2004 I survived a medical "odyssey." It caused me to rethink my life plan. What is success? What is important? I read the Ansdells' book. It helped me focus and develop a new life plan.

Barry Resnick, *Attorney*

I always wanted to read the Bible, but life kept getting in the way. The question and answer approach is great, and since I can do a few questions each day, I am actually doing it.

Paula Thomas, *Businesswoman*

It is a wonderful gift to be able to look at a book that is over 2000 years old and get excited about it all over again. Thank you for taking the time to make me want to look for answers in such a cheerful and fun-loving way.

Bridgette Cobb, *Professional photographer*

This book is a wonderful learning tool for my students and their budding faith and it has helped me notice things I hadn't understood before.

Stacy Walker, *Teacher*

The book is a gentle remiues of life and an appointment they   effective way to develop an appreci   Word.

Kay Comfort, *Author*

As a practicing Catholic I am now being encouraged to read the Bible, so this book excites me. I like the hunt it takes me on to find the answer; I also love gaining knowledge about what is found in the Scriptures.

Pat Dahl, *Bank representative*

Life insurance does not compare to the security and peace that Jesus Christ brings. This book helps you and your family to discuss, explore, and understand the Bible in a new way—and it's amazingly fun.

Richard Rey, *Insurance salesman*

1001
THINGS
You Should Know
Before You Die

by Allan & Yvonne Ansdell

Bridge-Logos
Alachua, Florida 32615

Bridge-Logos

Alachua, FL 32615 USA

1001 Things You Should Know Before You Die
by Allan and Yvonne Ansdell

Printed in the United States of America.

Library of Congress Catalog Card Number: 2007942783
International Standard Book Number 978-0-88270-470-8

Test Your Knowledge
Have Fun Finding the Answers!

Directions:

To find the answers, use your Bible (or purchase an easy-to-read, inexpensive paperback Bible) and mark it up as the answers jump out at you. Write your answers down in the spaces provided in this book.

Make it fun. You can do it yourself, ask a friend to join you, or get the whole family involved. The conversations will be very interesting. The answers will guide, encourage, fulfill, transform, educate you, and make a difference in your life.

Do a few questions each day and in no time you'll know why the Bible is known as "the greatest story ever told."

Log on to www.1001thingsyoushouldknow.org

As with the games "Jeopardy," "Wheel of Fortune," or crossword puzzles, everyone will have fun testing their skills and sharing their experience with others.

When we asked people to choose their favorite questions, we were surprised that they were all so different. Once you've finished this book, log on to our website, join our blog, and share your experience and insights with others. Let us know:

• What is your answer to the final question?
• How this book affected you and those you shared it with.
• Stories of faith and testimonies of life-changing events.

Each month we'll feature readers' inspiring reactions to this book, as well as comments from the authors and readers from around the world.

Matthew, Mark, Luke, and John are the authors of the first four books of the New Testament. Each recorded his eyewitness account of the same events from a different angle.

We will begin with the birth of Christ and continue through His childhood. This information is found in the first few chapters of Matthew and Luke.

Matthew: Chapter 1

Begin in verse 18 after the genealogy list.

1. Was Mary expecting a child before she was engaged to Joseph?

2. After Joseph found out Mary was "with child," what convinced him to not break off the engagement?

3. What reason was given to Joseph that the baby was special?

4. Why was the name Jesus chosen for the baby to come?

5. According to the "prophets of old," what set Mary's pregnancy apart from all others in history?

6. Did Joseph and Mary consummate their marriage before the birth of Christ?

Matthew: Chapter 2

7. What city was Jesus born in?

8. What prompted the wise men to come and worship Jesus?

9. Was it written in advance, by the prophets, exactly where the Christ child was to be born and what His purpose would be?

10. What gifts did the wise men bring the newborn Christ child?

11. Why did Joseph uproot his family and move them to Egypt, and what did this fulfill?

12. What did King Herod do to try and get rid of the Christ child?

13. Name the prophet from the Old Testament that describes King Herod's brutal actions?

14. If Jesus was born in Bethlehem, why was He called a Nazarene?

15. What was the significance of where Jesus grew up?

Now we will move forward to the book of Luke.
Luke recorded different details that will fill in the complete story
of the birth of Christ.

Luke: Chapter 1

16. Why did Luke say he wrote this account or summary of events?

17. What did the angel Gabriel tell Zechariah about his barren wife Elizabeth?

18. Why did Zechariah not believe what he was told by Gabriel?

19. What happened to the priest Zechariah because he did not believe the angel's words?

20. When the angel Gabriel visited the Virgin Mary, what was the first thing he told her?

21. What did the angel Gabriel tell Mary that caused her to question him?

22. What did the angel tell Mary about her conception?

23. Did Elizabeth acknowledge that her relative Mary was to be the mother of the Lord?

24. What event took place that gave Zechariah his voice back?

Luke: Chapter 2

25. What did Caesar Augustus command that caused everyone to return home to their own city or birthplace?

26. What city did Joseph and Mary return to?

27. When Jesus was born, what was He wrapped in?

28. Why was Jesus born in a manger?

29. Where were the shepherds and what were they doing when the angel of the Lord appeared to them?

30. What were the good tidings or news of great joy that the angel gave to the shepherds?

31. What information was given to the shepherds so they could recognize the Christ child?

32. Where did Mary store up the things being said about Jesus?

33. Where did Jesus grow up?

34. Joseph and Mary lost their young Jesus for three days. When they found Him what did He say?

Luke: Chapter 3

35. John baptized with water. What did he say the one mightier than he would baptize with?

36. After the baptism of Jesus, what did the voice from Heaven say?

37. How old was Jesus when He began His ministry?

Since Matthew, Mark, Luke, and John have similar content, we will fast forward to the book of John. Later we'll return to the other three books for additional insights.

John: Chapter 1

38. In the beginning what or who already existed?

39. The Scriptures say the Word was with God and the Word was
_____?

40. According to Scripture what gives someone the right to be called a child of God?

41. In the beginning was the Word. What became of the Word?

42. Quoting Isaiah, what did John the Baptist say his purpose was?

43. Who did John the Baptist proclaim Jesus to be?

44. What made John testify and acknowledge that Jesus was the Son of God?

John: Chapter 2

45. At the wedding in Cana what instructions did Jesus' mother Mary give to the servants?

46. What was the first miraculous thing Jesus did to make His disciples believe in Him?

47. What did Jesus say about merchants selling cattle, sheep, and doves in the temple?

48. What did Jesus mean when He said, "Destroy this temple, and I will raise it again in three days"?

John: Chapter 3

49. Who was Nicodemus?

50. When Nicodemus came to ask Jesus questions, what convinced him that God had sent Jesus to teach them?

51. In talking to Nicodemus, what did Jesus say must be done in order to see the Kingdom of God?

52. In John 3:16, what did God give to the world and why?

53. If God didn't send His son to condemn the world, why was He sent?

54. Some people will be judged or condemned, and others won't. Who will be judged?

55. Why do some people like the darkness rather than the light that came from Heaven?

56. What did John the Baptist say would happen to those who believed in Christ?

John: Chapter 4

57. When Jesus met the Samaritan woman at the well, why was she surprised that He talked to her?

58. How did Jesus say true worshipers will worship God?

59. When the Samaritan woman said she knew the Messiah would come and explain everything, what did Jesus tell her?

60. Where did Jesus say His food or nourishment came from?

John: Chapter 5

61. The Jews of that time were upset that Jesus had healed a man on the Sabbath, but what made them seek to kill him?

62. If you dishonor the Son who do you also dishonor?

63. How do you pass from death into life?

64. Did Jesus say the time is coming where everyone in the grave will hear His voice?

65. Jesus said He had a greater witness than John the Baptist that proved He was the Son of God. What was that proof?

66. When the Jews search the Old Testament Scriptures looking for eternal life, what does Jesus say the Scriptures actually do?

67. What person did Jesus say wrote about Him in the past?

John: Chapter 6

68. When Jesus fed the 5000, what did He do before He distributed the bread?

69. When Jesus walked on water to the boat and His disciples, how far from shore was it?

70. What did Jesus say people should be working for?

71. What did Jesus say was the work of God or what God wanted people to do?

72. What is the bread of God?

John: Chapter 7

73. Did Jesus' brothers believe in Him?

74. Why did Jesus say the world hates Him?

75. What would the people that believed in Christ receive and why had they not yet received it?

John: Chapter 8

76. When the leaders brought the woman caught in adultery to Jesus and asked whether they should stone her according to the law, what did Jesus tell them?

77. After saving the woman from being stoned what did Jesus command her to do?

78. For those that believed in Christ, what did He say they needed to do to be His disciples?

79. What did Jesus say about truth?

80. How does Jesus describe the devil?

81. What did Jesus say that caused the Jews to pick up stones to stone Him?

John: Chapter 9

82. When asked whether the sin of the blind man or his parents caused his blindness, what answer did Christ give?

83. What were the Jewish leaders of that day going to do to anyone who confessed a belief in Christ?

84. What did Christ tell the blind man when asked who is the Son of God?

John: Chapter 10

85. With Jesus as the Shepherd, who did He say would hear His voice?

86. In the shepherd's illustration, what did the thief come to do or what was his purpose?

87. What did Jesus say the Good Shepherd does for his sheep?

88. Jesus said He has the power or right to lay down His life voluntarily for the sheep, but He also had the power to do what?

89. When the Jews in the temple ask Jesus to tell them if He is the Christ, what did he say should have proven it to them?

90. After being asked by the leaders whether or not He was the Christ, what was the last thing Jesus said that caused them to pick up stones to stone Him?

John: Chapter 11

91. When Jesus was told about Lazarus being sick, what did He say about it?

92. What did Jesus tell Martha about the resurrection?

93. When Jesus commanded them to roll away the stone, how long did Martha say Lazarus had been dead?

94. When the chief Priests and Pharisees heard about Lazarus, what was their main concern would happen if everyone believed in Christ?

95. What actions did the Chief Priests and Pharisees decide to take after hearing about Lazarus?

John: Chapter 12

96. Mary poured perfume on Jesus feet. Why did He say she did it?

97. What did Judas do that showed his true character?

98. Why did the chief priests decide that Lazarus should also be put to death?

99. A huge crowd of Passover visitors went out to meet Christ. What did they bring with them?

100. What were the people shouting when they saw Jesus?

101. According to the Jewish leaders were many people following after Christ?

102. Many of the Jewish rulers believed in Christ, but why were they afraid to acknowledge it publicly?

103. Jesus said when you see him you actually see who?

104. Jesus said He is the light in the world. He said that people who believe in Him should not do what?

105. What will judge people in the last day?

John: Chapter 13

106. Who gave Judas the desire to betray Jesus?

107. What was Jesus trying to illustrate by taking on the job of a lowly servant and washing the feet of the disciples?

108. When Peter said he would lay down his life for Jesus, what did Jesus tell him?

John: Chapter 14

109. In Heaven, or the Father's house, who will prepare a place for believers?

110. How did Jesus say you can know the way to Heaven?

111. Did Jesus indicate there was any other way to the Father except through Him?

112. How did the apostles have such a great memory of everything that occurred and everything Jesus taught?

John: Chapter 15

113. God the Father is the gardener and we are the branches. What does the Father do to the branches that bear fruit or do not bear fruit?

114. What did Jesus say was the greatest love you could show your friends?

115. Why did Jesus say people no longer have an excuse for their sins?

116. Who is the counselor or helper Jesus sent to His disciples?

John: Chapter 16

117. Why did Jesus say it was best for His disciples that He leave them?

118. When the Counselor or Holy Spirit comes, why will the world be convicted of sin?

119. Jesus said His disciples were going to experience great sorrow at His departure but what would bring joy back to their hearts?

120. In the world the disciples were promised trials and tribulation but why were they encouraged to take heart or be of good cheer?

John: Chapter 17

121. Instead of praying to take believers out of the world, what did Jesus pray for them?

122. Jesus was praying for His disciples. He said He was also praying for who?

123. Who does the Father in Heaven love as much as He loves Christ?

John: Chapter 18

124. Who led the soldiers to arrest Christ?

125. How much did Jesus know about what was going to happen to Him?

126. When the soldiers said they wanted Jesus of Nazareth, and Jesus said, "I am He," what was their reaction?

127. What lie did Peter tell the servant girl in the courtyard?

128. What took place after Peter told his third lie as predicted by Christ?

129. After judging Jesus, what did Pilate say about his guilt or innocence?

130. When given an opportunity to release Christ what did the crowd do?

John: Chapter 19

131. After the soldiers put a crown of thorns on Jesus and mocked Him, what did they do to Him?

132. After Pilot told the chief priests that he found no fault with Jesus, why did they still want to put him to death?

133. What punishment did Pilate order for Christ?

134. What was the name of the place where Jesus was crucified?

135. What did the soldiers do that fulfilled an old prophecy?

136. What ladies were present and standing near the cross when Jesus was crucified?

137. What were Jesus' final words on the cross?

138. Why didn't the Jews want the bodies to remain on the cross?

139. The soldiers broke the legs of the two thieves. Why didn't they break the legs of Jesus?

140. What did one of the soldiers do to Jesus to make sure He was dead?

141. What were the results of this action?

142. Did the ancient Scriptures indicate that Jesus would not have any broken bones and that He would be pierced?

143. Who took the body of Jesus for burial?

144. What Jewish ruler brought the burial ointments?

145. Following the custom of the Jews for burial, what did they do to the body of Christ?

146. Where did they lay the body of Christ?

John: Chapter 20

147. What did Mary Magdalene find when she came to the tomb of Jesus?

148. When Mary told Peter about the missing body what did she think had happened?

149. What did Peter and the other disciple find when they entered the empty tomb?

150. When Mary Magdalene looked into the tomb, what did she see?

151. Who was the first person to see the resurrected Jesus?

152. Why did Jesus tell Mary not to cling to Him?

153. When Jesus appeared to the disciples, what did He show them?

154. Why did Jesus breathe on them?

155. When the disciples told Thomas they had seen the Lord what did Thomas say he would need to see and do?

156. When the Lord had Thomas look at His hands and put his hand in His side, what did Thomas say?

157. Jesus told Thomas, "Because you have seen me, you have believed." What did He say about the ones who have *not* seen Him yet they believe?

158. Were all the miracles done by Christ written in this book of John?

159. Why did the author John say he recorded the miracles of Christ?

John: Chapter 21

160. On His third visit after being raised from the dead, what did Jesus do for the disciples?

161. After Peter told Jesus that he loved Him more than anyone, what did Jesus ask Him to do?

162. How did the author John describe the amount of books that could be written about what Jesus did?

Acts: Chapter 1

163. During the 40 days after His crucifixion what was Christ showing the apostles about himself?

164. The apostles were told by Jesus not to leave Jerusalem until what happened to them?

165. When the apostles were on the Mount of Olives, what miraculous way did Jesus leave them?

166. Talking to the apostles, how did the men dressed in white robes say Jesus would return?

167. How many apostles were there at this time?

168. When the apostles went to the upper room, who joined them in prayer?

169. What is the field called where Judas died?

170. What attributes did the candidates to replace Judas have in common with the other apostles?

171. What is the name of the apostle who replaced Judas?

Acts: Chapter 2

172. The believers were filled with the Holy Spirit on the day of _____?

173. What abilities were given to the group of believers when they were filled with the Spirit?

174. When the Jews from many nations living in Jerusalem encountered the believers what astonished them?

175. Which ancient prophet from the Old Testament said that after God's Spirit was poured out upon the people "everyone who calls on the name of the Lord will be saved"?

176. What ancient Jewish King predicted that God would not let His Holy one decay in the grave?

177. After Peter told a group of Jews that they had actually crucified the long awaited Christ, what did he say they should do?

178. What did believers do to help other believers in need?

Acts: Chapter 3

179. When the man who was crippled from birth asked Peter and John for money what did they tell him?

180. What was God's promise to Abraham?

Acts: Chapter 4

181. What surprised the Jewish leaders about Peter and John's abilities?

182. Why couldn't the leaders deny that a miracle had truly taken place with the lame man?

Acts: Chapter 5

183. When talking to Peter, what did a believer do that caused the believer to drop dead?

184. Peter told the believer who lied about his donation that he didn't lie to men but to who?

185. When all the apostles were put in jail, who released them and for what reason?

186. Why did Gamaliel advise the Jewish council not to kill the apostles?

187. After being beaten and told by the Jewish council not to speak in the name of Jesus again, why did the apostles rejoice?

Acts: Chapter 6

188. The Scriptures say that the Word of God spread and the number of believers multiplied greatly. Who did they say were included in that number?

Acts: Chapter 7

189. In Stephen's review of the Jewish history, who did God give the covenant of circumcision to?

190. How old was Moses when his parents had to abandon him?

191. Who found baby Moses and took care of him?

192. After fleeing Egypt and living in Midian, how many years passed before the angel in the flaming bush appeared to Moses?

193. What was the location where Moses encountered the angel in the burning bush?

194. When the Jews had made a golden calf as an idol, what did God give them up to do?

195. What does the prophet from the Old Testament say about God's need for a house or temple?

196. After Stephen's oration of the Jewish history, what did he accuse the Jewish leaders of doing that their ancestors had done?

197. When Stephen gazed into Heaven, what did he proclaim?

198. When they stoned Stephen, where did they lay their coats?

199. When Stephen was calling on God to receive his spirit, what did he ask for those who were stoning him?

Acts: Chapter 8

200. Who created havoc for the believers, taking men and women to prison?

201. What did the sorcerer do that made Peter so mad?

202. What book of the Old Testament was the Ethiopian having trouble understanding   when Philip encountered him?

203. What are the first two lines of the Scripture that Philip helped the Ethiopian to understand?

204. What did the Ethiopian do after he was convinced that Jesus Christ is the son of God?

Acts: Chapter 9

205. As Saul journeyed to Damascus, what caused him to fall to the ground?

206. When Saul heard a voice from Heaven, what was the question asked of him?

207. Who did the voice Saul heard on the road to Damascus identify himself to be?

208. When the Lord told Ananias in a vision to go to Saul and put a hand on him to give him sight, why was Ananias concerned?

209. How did the Lord reassure Ananias about going to see Saul?

210. What happened to Saul after Ananias laid hands on him and what did Saul then do?

211. When the Jews tried to kill Saul, how did the disciples save him?

212. Why wouldn't the disciples allow Saul to join them?

213. In the town of Joppa, what was the name of the female disciple who died and was raised by Peter's prayers?

Acts: Chapter 10

214. When Peter was on the roof top and had a vision, what was it he saw?

215. What did the voice that came to Peter during the vision command him to do?

216. What was Peter's argument for not doing what he was told to do during the vision?

217. What was God's response to Peter's refusal to follow this command?

218. When Cornelius the centurion fell at the feet of Peter to worship him, what did Peter tell him?

219. Peter told Cornelius that it was unlawful for a Jew to enter the home of a Gentile, but through his vision what did he learn from God?

220. After preaching Jesus to the household of Cornelius, what was the main thing about them receiving the Holy Spirit that astonished Peter's friends?

Acts: Chapter 11

221. When Peter told the apostles about the vision and his right to enter a Gentile's house, what final statement did he make that convinced them it was okay?

222. In what city were the disciples first called Christians?

Acts: Chapter 12

223. After King Herod had killed the brother of John why did he have Peter seized?

224. When Peter was chained between two guards, what happened when the angel told him to rise up?

225. When Herod searched the prison for Peter and could not find him, what action did he take?

Acts: Chapter 13

226. What name was Saul also known as?

227. When Saul was reviewing the Jewish history in the synagogue, what did he say God said about King David?

228. What did God say about Jesus in the second Psalm?

229. After Paul and Barnabus explained the necessity of giving the good news to the Jews first what did he say the Lord now commanded them to do?

Acts: Chapter 14

230. When Paul saw the man crippled from birth, why did He think this man could receive a healing?

231. In Lystra after Paul healed a man, what did the people do that caused both Paul and Barnabas to tear their clothing?

232. In earlier days God allowed nations to walk their own way but always left a witness and reminders of himself. What were some of these reminders?

Acts: Chapter 15

233. What did some of the believing Pharisees want the Gentiles to do in order to be part of the church?

234. In a letter what did the apostles instruct the new believing Gentiles to do?

Acts: Chapter 16

235. After Paul caused the spirit of fortune telling to come out of the slave girl, why were her masters so upset?

236. After Paul was imprisoned and the jail keeper found the doors of the prison open from the earthquake, why was the jailer going to take his own life?

237. When the jailer found Paul and Silas, what did he ask them?

238. After refusing to be let out of prison by the magistrates, what did Paul tell them that caused them to be afraid?

Acts: Chapter 17

239. What action did the Jews take because they were jealous and not persuaded by Paul's speech?

240. When Paul was teaching in Athens, what troubled him about the city?

241. What was the main past-time of the people of Athens?

242. What was the inscription on the altar that Paul used as his example when talking to the council in Athens?

243. How did Paul describe the men of Athens?

244. What was the reason given by Paul that God didn't need temples or things made by man?

Acts: Chapter 18

245. What was Paul's trade?

246. When the Jews opposed Paul and insulted him in Corinth, what did he tell them?

247. What was the theme of the message God gave to Paul in a vision when he was in Corinth?

Acts: Chapter 19

248. Did the people in Asia hear about the Lord's message?

249. Some exorcists decided to use the name Jesus to rid people of evil spirits; when they did this, what was the reply of the evil spirit?

250. What did many of the people who practiced magic (or sorcery) do after seeing what was happening with evil spirits?

251. Why did Demetrius the silversmith dislike the fact that Paul was converting people to Christianity?

Acts: Chapter 20

252. Paul said his life was worth nothing unless he used it for the work assigned him by the Lord Jesus. What was that assignment?

253. When Paul was saying that he provided necessities for himself and his friends, what quote did he give from the Lord Jesus?

Acts: Chapter 21

254. Paul was not afraid of a statement made by Agabus, but instead he was ready to do what for Christ?

255. When the Jews from Asia stirred up the crowd what did they say Paul had done that defiled the temple?

256. When the commander rescued Paul from being beaten to death by the crowd what language did Paul use to speak to him?

257. What language did Paul use to speak to the crowd, and what effect did it have on them?

Acts: Chapter 22

258. Why did the crowd interrupt Paul and say he should not be allowed to live?

259. What did Paul tell those arresting him that caused all of them, including the commander, to fear?

Acts: Chapter 23

260. When Paul was brought before the council, what did he say that caused dissension among the council members?

261. What is the difference between a Pharisee and a Sadducee?

262. After being moved to the barracks what did the Lord tell Paul that was to encourage him?

263. Over 40 Jews banded together and took an oath. What was that oath?

264. To what governor did the commander send Paul?

Acts: Chapter 24

265. Paul said he had hope in God. What did that hope include?

266. The governor held Paul for over 2 years. During that time what was he hoping Paul would do?

Acts: Chapter 25

267. While on trial to whom did Paul say he wanted to appeal?

Acts: Chapter 26

268. When Paul was giving his defense to King Agrippa what was the quote he gave from Moses?

269. When King Agrippa and Festus talked, what did they say would have happened if Paul had not appealed to Caesar?

Acts: Chapter 27

270. When Paul was caught in a violent storm on a ship being sent to Rome, what did he tell the crew when he addressed them?

271. Did all the men survive the shipwreck, and how many were there?

Acts: Chapter 28

272. What happened to Paul when he put a bundle of sticks on the fire?

273. What did the natives think when they saw this happen to Paul?

274. What did Paul do for the islanders that encouraged them to supply all his crew's needs for their voyage?

275. While in Rome was Paul allowed to live all alone?

276. When Paul, using the Prophets and the Law of Moses, testified to the leaders of the Jews, did they all believe?

277. Paul talked with the Jewish leaders, some believed and some did not. Paul quoted Isaiah to them. What is the main theme of this prophecy?

Romans: Chapter 1

278. What was the proof that Jesus was the Son of God?

279. Why did Paul want to visit the believers in Rome whom he prayed for continually?

280. What does God in Heaven show His anger against?

281. What do the people who are the target of God's anger do to the truth?

282. Do people have an excuse for not knowing God, and why?

283. Paul says that although people knew God, what didn't they do?

284. Even though ungodly people claim to be wise and knowledgeable, what does the Bible actually say about them?

285. If man chooses to be unrighteous, what does God do about it?

286. Since ungodly men gave up the truth of God for a lie, what did they worship?

287. When people are doing wrong in God's eyes what do they encourage others to do?

Romans: Chapter 2

288. What are the ungodly storing up for themselves in the future?

289. How will God, the just judge of all the world, judge all people?

290. Who will God give eternal life to?

291. Who will God pour out His wrath and anger on?

292. Does God show favoritism or partiality to anyone?

293. What is more important than knowing God's law?

294. How can those who rely on their knowledge of God's law actually dishonor God?

295. How do the Scriptures describe a true Jew?

296. What kind of inward circumcision does God's Spirit perform?

Romans: Chapter 3

297. What was the advantage of being a Jew?

298. What do both Jews and Gentiles have in common?

299. What is the purpose of the Law (the 10 commandments)?

300. How are we made right or justified in God's eyes?

301. Is man justified by his good deeds or by observing the law?

Romans: Chapter 4

302. Who was the father of the Jewish nation?

303. What did Abraham do to be considered righteous by God?

304. Abraham's circumcision was proof of what?

305. Why did God's promise to Abraham to have children seem impossible to fulfill?

306. What do we have to do to be considered righteous by God?

307. What two things did Jesus do to get rid of our offenses or sins and to present us as justified or right with God?

Romans: Chapter 5

308. What benefit do we have from being made right with God?

309. Why would we ever rejoice when we run into problems?

310. If you had the opportunity to die for a good person, you may or may not, but what did Christ do that shows God's great love for us?

311. Since we have been made right in God's sight by the blood of Christ, will He save us from judgment?

312. When Adam sinned what were the two long-range effects on the human race?

Romans: Chapter 6

313. What does Paul imply that is characteristic about the life of someone who has died to sin?

314. How is a person symbolically buried with Christ?

315. When Christ rose from the dead, what happened to death?

316. What should a person do that has died to sin?

317. What do you receive as wages or earnings for sin?

318. When God gives you eternal life, is it considered something earned or a gift?

Romans: Chapter 7

319. Why does the law no longer hold a believer in its power?

320. How should the believer who has been delivered from the law serve God?

321. If you do something against your will, what causes you to do that?

Romans: Chapter 8

322. Name one of the benefits for those that belong to Christ?

323. Why could the law not save us?

324. There is a difference between a carnal (or sinful) mind and a spiritual mind. What are the differences?

325. Who is it that can never please God?

326. Does a believer have the same spirit Christ has in Him?

327. What happens to a believer if he or she keeps on following their sinful ways?

328. What qualifies a person to be considered a son of God?

329. Who can pray for a believer when they do not know what to pray?

330. What comfort can God give a believer when things aren't going right in their lives?

331. What are some of the things that cannot separate a believer from Christ?

Romans: Chapter 9

332. To what extreme would Paul go to, if possible, to bring salvation to his Jewish brothers and sisters?

333. What did God choose to do through Pharaoh?

334. Why did Paul say we don't have the right to question God?

335. In quoting Hosea, what did God proclaim about those who were not His people?

336. In quoting Isaiah did God indicate how many people of Israel will be saved?

Romans: Chapter 10

337. Exactly how can you be saved?

338. Who can be saved, or is salvation for just a select few?

339. What produces faith or how does it "come"?

Romans: Chapter 11

340. What was one of the things Paul was hoping to do by working with the Gentiles?

341. What example did Paul use to illustrate how a new believer becomes part of the Jewish family?

342. Why should believers not brag about their new position in the Jewish family?

343. What will it take for Jewish people to be grafted back into God's family tree?

344. Why can we not question the judgments of God?

Romans: Chapter 12

345. What does Paul say we should do with our bodies?

346. If a believer is not to conform to the ways of this world, how are they supposed to change?

347. How does God look at us as a family?

348. What are some of the gifts and abilities God gives to people?

349. What should you do when someone persecutes you?

350. How should you show compassion to other people during good or bad times?

351. How should a believer act around other people?

352. How do you conquer evil?

Romans: Chapter 13

353. What does God say about taxes?

354. What is the one debt that you never finish paying off?

355. What is the one thing you must do to fulfill all the requirements of the law?

356. How does God say we should live our lives?

Romans: Chapter 14

357. How should you respect a Christian who is weak in the faith?

358. The Scriptures indicate we will all do what before God's judgment seat?

359. Does the Scripture say that each of us will give an account of ourselves to God?

360. If Paul says that all foods are acceptable to eat, when should you not eat a particular food?

Romans: Chapter 15

361. Why did Paul want to preach where no other person had yet preached?

Romans: Chapter 16

362. Who did Paul warn the church to watch out for?

First Corinthians: Chapter 1

363. What did Christ send Paul out to do?

364. To some the message of the cross is foolishness and to others it demonstrates the power of God. Who are these two groups?

365. What will God do with the wisdom of the wise?

366. Will man, through his own wisdom, know God?

367. What did God do so that no one could glory or boast in his presence?

First Corinthians: Chapter 2

368. What do Scriptures say that man has never seen nor heard?

369. It's impossible to know another man because we don't have his spirit. How can we know God?

370. Why does a non Christian, a natural man, not receive the things of the Spirit of God?

371. Why does the Bible say that Christians can understand the Spirit of God?

First Corinthians: Chapter 3

372. When Paul spoke to new Christians in Corinth, in what way did he say he had to speak to them?

373. What was the analogy that Paul used to explain the teamwork between the apostles and God?

374. Paul tells the Corinthian believers that they are God's building. What do they need as a foundation for them to remain standing?

375. In Paul's analogy how will every person's works be tested?

376. Paul describes Christians as being temples. What is unique about this temple?

First Corinthians: Chapter 4

377. Why should people not be boastful about their talents?

378. What are some of the things Paul says he and the Apostles endured in order to preach the gospel?

First Corinthians: Chapter 5

379. Is it acceptable for Christians to keep company with an immoral person who doesn't claim to be a Christian?

First Corinthians: Chapter 6

380. What do the Scriptures say about lawsuits, with Christians suing Christians?

381. Who are some of the people listed in Scripture that will not inherit the Kingdom of God?

382. Why should you honor God with your body by not committing sexual sins?

First Corinthians: Chapter 7

383. If a Christian man or woman is married to a non Christian and the non Christian wants to leave the marriage, what should they do?

First Corinthians: Chapter 8

384. What was Paul's attitude about anything that caused another Christian to stumble?

First Corinthians: Chapter 9

385. Why did Paul refuse to take money for preaching?

386. In the Scriptures Paul talks about running a race. How does he say you must run and what is your prize?

First Corinthians: Chapter 10

387. What caused 23,000 Israelites to die in one day?

388. What was the purpose of so many Israelites dying?

389. What two things will God do for you when temptation comes into your life?

390. How should a Christian act toward other Christians?

First Corinthians: Chapter 11

391. On the night Jesus was betrayed, He used bread and wine as an example of what?

392. What did Jesus say should be the purpose of participating in the ceremony known as communion?

First Corinthians: Chapter 12

393. The Scriptures say that there are different kinds of spiritual gifts that are given to believers. What do they all have in common?

394. What is meant by "the body of Christ"?

395. How is the body of Christ affected when one member is honored or suffers?

396. What are some of the members that make up the body of Christ?

First Corinthians: Chapter 13

397. What are some of the qualities of love?

398. Believers are to abide in faith, hope and love, but the greatest of these is what?

First Corinthians: Chapter 14

399. If a person has the ability to speak in an unknown language (tongues), who are they talking to?

400. What do the Scriptures say spiritual gifts should be used for?

First Corinthians: Chapter 15

401. How did Paul sum up the "good news" or the Gospel of Christ?

402. After Christ was raised from the dead, how many people saw him at one time (other than the apostles)?

403. Why did Paul consider himself to be the least of the apostles?

404. If Christ did not rise from the dead, what do Scriptures say about the Christian faith?

405. If Christ did not rise from the dead then what has happened to all those people who have "died in their sins"?

406. Death came into the world through what man?

407. The resurrection from the dead began through what man?

408. What is the order in which everyone will be resurrected?

409. When Christ brings an end to the world, what will He do?

410. What is the last enemy that Christ will destroy?

411. What does evil company corrupt?

412. In Paul's analogy about the resurrection of the dead, what must happen to a planted seed before it produces life?

413. Once the natural body is buried, how is it raised?

414. What was the first man, Adam, made of?

415. What will happen at the sound of the last trumpet?

416. What did Paul say to encourage and strengthen the believers in their work for the Lord?

First Corinthians: Chapter 16

417. How did Paul say you should greet one another?

Second Corinthians: Chapter 1

418. When God comforts us in our tribulations, what does that give us the ability to do?

419. Christ has sealed believers and given them a deposit. What is that deposit?

Second Corinthians: Chapter 2

420. Was Paul concerned that Satan could take advantage of him or others?

421. Believers are the fragrance of Christ to what two groups of people?

422. The aroma or fragrance of Christ is different to each group, describe the difference?

423. Did Paul acknowledge that even in his day some people peddled the Word of God?

Second Corinthians: Chapter 3

424. Why could the people of Israel not understand what was being read from the Old Testament?

425. How can the veil that keeps the children of Israel from understanding the Old Testament be taken away?

Second Corinthians: Chapter 4

426. Who is the gospel veiled to or hidden from?

427. Who has blinded the eyes of the unbelievers?

428. Why were the eyes of the unbelievers blinded?

429. Why does Paul not lose heart even though his outward body is perishing?

Second Corinthians: Chapter 5

430. When our earthly tent or body is taken away in death, will it be replaced?

431. What will our earthly tent or body be replaced with?

432. What has God done to guarantee us new bodies and everlasting life?

433. If you are a believer and absent from this earthly body, where will you be?

434. Whether in this body or our future eternal body, what should be our aim or goal?

435. Where does the Word of God say we must all stand or appear when this life is over?

436. How does the Bible describe a person who is in Christ or a Christian?

437. What does the Bible say has happened to a believer's life?

438. Are all believers reconciled (brought back to God) through Christ without having their sins counted against them?

439. What did God do about our sin that would make us righteous in His eyes?

Second Corinthians: Chapter 6

440. As God's workers or partners, what did Paul plead with us not to do?

441. What day does the Bible say is the day of salvation?

442. What does the Bible say about the relationship between believers and unbelievers?

443. What does God say takes place if you are His temple?

Second Corinthians: Chapter 7

444. After receiving all of God's promises, what are we told to do?

445. There is godly sorrow and there is worldly sorrow (sorrow without repentance). What is the difference between the two?

Second Corinthians: Chapter 8

446. Why does the Bible say that Christ gave up His riches to become poor?

447. Paul sent a partner or spiritual brother to the Corinthians and then had one of his letters named after that man. What is the name of that person?

Second Corinthians: Chapter 9

448. Concerning the giving of money, what does the Bible say about sowing and reaping (planting and harvesting)?

449. God doesn't want us to give grudgingly or in response to pressure. How does He want us to give?

450. How does God bless you when you give?

Second Corinthians: Chapter 10

451. The Scriptures say that if you glory (boast), you should glory in what?

Second Corinthians: Chapter 11

452. What concerned Paul about the Corinthians?

453. How does the Bible say Satan can disguise himself?

454. The Bible says that even Satan's ministers can pretend to be what?

Second Corinthians: Chapter 12

455. What did Paul witness 14 years before he wrote this letter to the Corinthians?

456. What happened to Paul to make sure he didn't become exalted or puffed up?

457. How many times did Paul plead with the Lord to be healed?

458. What was the Lord's two-fold response to Paul's request for healing?

459. Why could Paul be content or actually take pleasure in his infirmities?

460. Paul said he didn't want what the Corinthians had. What did He want?

461. What are some of the things Paul was afraid he might find when he came back to the Corinthians?

Second Corinthians: Chapter 13

462. Quoting the Old Testament, what did Paul say establishes a case against someone?

463. Why did Paul want the Corinthians to examine themselves?

464. What did Paul say it means if Jesus couldn't be detected among the Corinthian people?

Galatians: Chapter 1

465. Paul was an apostle appointed by whom and why?

466. Was it part of God's plan that Jesus would give Himself for our sins?

467. What shocked Paul about the Churches of the Galatians?

468. What were the people who were troubling or fooling the Galatians trying to do?

469. The Scriptures say to let God's curse fall on anyone, including Paul, or even an angel, if they do what?

470. According to Paul, if he were trying to please men, what did that say about him?

471. Where did Paul say he received his information for preaching?

472. In his former life as a Jew, what did Paul try to do about Christians?

473. After three years who did Paul visit in Jerusalem, and for how long?

474. What were the churches in Judea hearing about Paul?

Galatians: Chapter 2

475. God gave Paul the responsibility of preaching to whom?

476. Name the apostles who were considered to be the pillars of the church?

477. Why did Paul accuse Peter of being a hypocrite?

478. Paul acknowledged with Peter that they were both Jews and followers of the law. What did he say the law was unable to do for them?

479. Why did Paul say that he died to the law?

480. Paul said that he was crucified with Christ. How did he complete this statement?

481. If righteousness comes by the law, then did Christ's death serve a purpose?

Galatians: Chapter 3

482. Did God do miracles among the people of Galatia because of the Law of Moses or their faith?

483. Since Abraham was considered righteous because of his faith, who does the Bible say are the sons (or children) of Abraham?

484. Quoting a passage from Deuteronomy and Habakkuk, why are those who depend on the law for justification cursed?

485. Who has rescued us from the curse of the law and how?

486. How many years after God's promise or covenant with Abraham were the 10 commandments (the law) given to Moses?

487. The purpose of the 10 commandments was to show us how guilty we are. What is its other function?

488. In Christ is there equality for people of all nations, genders and social classes?

Galatians: Chapter 4

489. According to God's Word, if we are no longer slaves, or outsiders, but adopted as sons of God through Christ, then what are we entitled to?

490. The Galatians had compassion for Paul's infirmity; in fact he said that if they could they would even do what for him?

491. How many sons did Abraham have and who were their mothers?

492. How did each of Abraham's sons differ?

Galatians: Chapter 5

493. What does God's Word say it means to have "fallen from grace"?

494. What do the Scriptures say that believers should *not* do with their new freedom or liberty in Christ?

495. The whole law can be summed up in this one command, what is it?

496. If you are not to do what your sinful nature craves, what must you do?

497. What is the constant battle that goes on within a believer?

498. List some of the actions that are evidence of the lust of the flesh or a person's sinful nature?

499. What will happen to people who continually practice sin, and follow their lustful flesh?

500. What are the nine fruits of the Spirit?

501. A person who belongs to Christ has crucified what?

502. If we live in the Spirit and walk in the Spirit, what three things do the Scriptures say we are not to do?

Galatians: Chapter 6

503. What does God's word say we should do for a person who is overcome by a sin?

504. The Bible says not to be deceived and that God will not be mocked. How does it describe sowing and reaping?

505. If you live to satisfy your sinful pleasures (sowing to the flesh), what will be the consequences?

506. If you live to please the Spirit of God, what are you promised?

Ephesians: Chapter 1

507. Who was the letter of Ephesians sent to?

508. What is the status of the believers who were chosen by God before the world was created?

509. What do we have in Christ through His blood?

510. What is the purpose of the believer being sealed with the Holy Spirit of promise?

511. What was Paul's prayer for the believers?

512. When God raised Christ from the dead what did God do with all worldly power and authority?

Ephesians: Chapter 2

513. How is the prince of this world described?

514. Where does this prince do his work?

515. When God saves a person by grace or special favor, what do you call it?

516. Why does the Bible say God did not save anyone through works or special deeds?

517. Since Christians are Gods workmanship and masterpiece what were they created for in Christ?

518. What has Christ done for both the Jews and Gentiles?

Ephesians: Chapter 3

519. What secrets or mysteries were revealed to the apostles and prophets that were not previously revealed to past generations?

520. When Paul prayed for believers, what did he say about the depth or measure of Christ's love?

521. With the amazing power of the Spirit that works in the believer what is God able to do for their prayers and requests?

Ephesians: Chapter 4

522. Does the Bible say there is more than one Lord or one faith or even one Father in Heaven?

523. The Scriptures say that the believer should no longer be like children, in what way?

524. What does the Bible say to do about your anger?

525. What is said in the Word about the reason to work or labor?

526. What does the Bible say about how to talk or communicate?

527. Rather than being bitter, full of anger, or using harsh words and slander, what would the Word of God have you do?

Ephesians: Chapter 5

528. In the Scriptures believers are described as being once in darkness and now in the light. What are they now to do about the unfruitful deeds of darkness?

529. Walking circumspectly or in attentive wisdom, how are believers supposed to spend their time?

530. What should you give thanks for to God in the name of Jesus?

531. In a Christian marriage if a husband is to be head of the wife as Christ is the head of the church, what is the wife supposed to do?

532. In return what's the example of the type of love a husband is to have for his wife?

533. Paul quotes a passage from Genesis about when a man leaves his father and mother and is joined to his wife. What happens to the two when they are joined?

Ephesians: Chapter 6

534. Regarding children, what is the first commandment with a promise, and what is that promise?

535. How are fathers to raise their children?

536. What should be the manner in which a servant or employee works for his boss?

537. What should a boss keep in mind in respect to those he has employed?

538. Why should a person put on the whole armor of God?

539. When putting on the whole armor of God, if it is not for fighting against flesh and blood what is it for?

540. Using the example of armor, what should you wrap around your waist?

541. What should you put over your chest?

542. What should you put on for shoes?

543. What will stop the fiery darts of Satan known as the wicked one?

544. What do you cover your head with?

545. What is to be used as your weapon (the sword of the spirit)?

546. What was the main thing Paul wanted the church to pray for him?

Philippians: Chapter 1

547. What will God do for a Christian once He has started a good work in him?

548. What benefit did Paul say was derived from the trials that he endured?

549. How did the fact that Paul was in chains help his brethren?

550. How did Paul feel about the fact that some preached Christ out of selfish ambition and some out of love?

551. How did Paul personally feel about dying?

552. What did Paul tell the Philippians they would be granted or privileged to do for Christ?

Philippians: Chapter 2

553. The Bible says not to do things out of selfish ambition, so what are you supposed to do?

554. Since Christ was equal to God, what did He do that was so humbling?

555. As a servant what was Christ's final act of obedience?

556. Who did the Bible say would bow at the name of Jesus?

557. What does the Word of God say every tongue will confess?

558. Why does the Bible say it is best to do things without murmuring or arguing?

Philippians: Chapter 3

559. In Paul's genealogy what Jewish tribe or family was he from?

560. Now that Paul had the knowledge of Christ, how did he sum up his past status and accomplishments?

561. Where did Paul say he now holds his citizenship?

Philippians: Chapter 4

562. In what book were the names of Paul's fellow workers written?

563. What does the Lord want us to do about anxiety or worry?

564. When we turn our concerns over to God and let our requests be known through prayer, what does God do for us?

565. What are Christian believers told to meditate on?

566. Paul learned how to be content in any condition. How?

Colossians: Chapter 1

567. What is Christ the visible image of?

568. Who is the first born from the dead?

569. How did God make peace with everything in Heaven and on Earth?

570. How are believers presented to God now that Christ has reconciled them through His death?

571. What does the Bible say is your part in this presentation?

Colossians: Chapter 2

572. What does the Bible say that believers should beware of (to avoid being taken captive)?

573. For believers, what was previously against them that has been cancelled, wiped out, and nailed to the cross?

Colossians: Chapter 3

574. What should believers set their minds on?

575. How should your manner of work be?

Colossians: Chapter 4

576. How should Christians treat non-Christians?

First Thessalonians: Chapter 1

577. Paul said that their gospel didn't come to the Thessalonians in word only. How else did it come to them?

First Thessalonians: Chapter 2

578. Who prevented Paul from coming to the Thessalonians?

First Thessalonians: Chapter 3

579. Why did Paul send Timothy to the church in Thessalonica?

First Thessalonians: Chapter 4

580. What does the Bible say will happen to those who have died or sleep in Jesus?

581. When the Lord himself descends from Heaven, who will rise first and who will follow?

582. What will happen to believers who are alive on the Earth when the Lord returns?

First Thessalonians: Chapter 5

583. What description was used to describe how or when the Lord would return?

584. How should we pray?

585. What are believers told to stay away from?

Second Thessalonians: Chapter 1

586. When the Lord Jesus is revealed from Heaven with His mighty angels, who will He take vengeance or judgment on?

587. How will these people be punished?

Second Thessalonians: Chapter 2

588. What must happen before the Lord returns?

589. What will the son of perdition or the man of lawlessness do when he is revealed?

590. How will the lawless one be destroyed?

591. When the lawless one comes how does he do the work of Satan?

592. Why is the lawless one able to deceive those who are perishing?

593. Those who did not believe in Christ took pleasure in or enjoyed doing what?

First Timothy: Chapter 1

594. Why does the Word say not to pay heed to fables or endless genealogies?

595. Name some of the things that are contrary to sound doctrine or good teaching?

596. Christ Jesus came into the world to save sinners. Who did Paul say was the chief sinner?

First Timothy: Chapter 2

597. What is God's desire for all men?

598. There is one God and one Mediator. Who does the Bible say is the mediator between men and God?

599. Regarding Adam and Eve, who was deceived first?

First Timothy: Chapter 3

600. What does the Bible say can cause a Bishop or an Elder of a church to fall?

601. What are some of the godly qualifications of a bishop or deacon?

602. What is the description of Christ outlined in Chapter 3?

First Timothy: Chapter 4

603. What is better than physical exercise and what does it promise us?

First Timothy: Chapter 6

604. What does the Bible say about possessions?

605. What does the Word say can happen to a person who desires to be rich?

606. People say "money is the root of all evil." What does the complete Scripture actually say?

607. What instructions or command does the Bible give to the rich?

608. What final instructions did Paul give Timothy about what to avoid?

Second Timothy: Chapter 1

609. If God has not given us a spirit of fear then what spirit has He given us?

610. What did Jesus do with death and life?

Second Timothy: Chapter 2

611. What does a good soldier of Jesus Christ do?

612. If you are engaged in warfare how should you act?

613. How does an athlete compete for the crown?

614. What are hardworking farmers entitled to?

615. In his chains what did Paul say about the Word of God?

616. Why should a believer avoid foolish arguments?

617. What should be the qualities of those who serve the Lord?

Second Timothy: Chapter 3

618. In the last days what are some of the things that will be taking place?

619. When you desire to live a godly life in Christ, what will you suffer?

620. Were the Scriptures written by man's inspiration?

621. What is Scripture profitable or useful for?

622. What does a person gain by knowing the Scriptures?

Second Timothy: Chapter 4

623. The time will come when people will no longer listen to sound teaching. What will they do?

Titus: Chapter 1

624. There are people who claim to know God but really don't. What behavior characterizes such people?

Titus: Chapter 2

625. What are some of the things Paul said older women should teach the younger women?

Titus: Chapter 3

626. What did Paul say Titus should avoid and why?

Philemon: Chapter 1

627. What did Paul ask Philemon to do for his new son from prison and what request was for himself?

Hebrews: Chapter 1

628. God spoke to the Jewish ancestors in the past through prophets. What was the final way He spoke to us?

629. In Hebrews how is Christ's image described?

630. What does the Bible say will happen to the heavens and the Earth?

631. According to the Bible what is the job description of an angel?

Hebrews: Chapter 2

632. Who held the power of death that Christ by His death destroyed?

Hebrews: Chapter 3

633. Today if you hear the voice of God what should you *not* do?

Hebrews: Chapter 4

634. What is sharper than a two-edged sword?

635. The Word of God is powerful enough to do what?

636. What gives Jesus the ability to sympathize with our weaknesses?

Hebrews: Chapter 5

637. What purpose does the Jewish high priest serve?

638. Why does a priest have compassion for others' weaknesses?

639. How did Christ as the Son of God learn obedience?

640. Describe a Christian who is able to have solid food as opposed to milk?

Hebrews: Chapter 6

641. If a field bears a useless crop, what does the farmer do to the crop?

642. When God takes an oath, who does He swear by?

Hebrews: Chapter 7

643. Melchizedek was the king of what city?

644. In what way does Melchizedek resemble the Son of God?

645. What did Abraham do that acknowledged how great a man Melchizedek was?

646. Who is greater, the one with the power to bless or the one being blessed?

Hebrews: Chapter 8

647. Where is Christ, the High Priest, seated in Heaven?

Hebrews: Chapter 9

648. The tabernacle (sacred tent) had two rooms. What three things were in the first room called the sanctuary or holy place?

649. What separated the second room, called the Most Holy Place, from the Holy Place?

650. What was in the second room that only the High Priest could enter?

651. What did the High Priest take into the Most Holy Place, once a year, as a sacrifice for himself and all the people?

652. Christ did not offer the blood of goats or calves, like the Jewish high priest, but rather His own. What did He obtain with this offering?

653. How often will a man die?

654. What happens after death?

Hebrews: Chapter 11

655. How is faith described in the Word of God?

656. What does the Bible say visible things of the universe are made of?

657. What must you have to please God?

658. Noah built an ark on faith. What was unusual about the warning that caused him to build this ark?

659. What did all these people have in common? Abel, Enoch, Noah, Abraham, Sarah, Isaac, Jacob, Joseph, Moses.

660. Did all the people of faith receive their final promise yet?

Hebrews: Chapter 12

661. According to the Scriptures in Hebrews, how should we run the race that is set before us?

662. Why was Jesus willing to endure the cross?

663. When you become weary and discouraged what should you think about?

664. Why should you not despise discipline by the Lord or be discouraged by it?

665. What does it mean if you are not disciplined by the Lord?

666. What did Esau sell for food?

Hebrews: Chapter 13

667. Why does the Bible say to show hospitality to strangers?

668. Which sentence tells you whether Jesus ever changes?

James: Chapter 1

669. When you fall into various troubles (or face trials), how can you call it all joy?

670. If you need wisdom what should you do?

671. What will God do if you ask for wisdom?

672. What attitude do you need to assure that the Lord will answer your prayers?

673. What will happen to the accomplishments and pursuits of the rich man?

674. Why is a person blessed who endures temptation (or perseveres under trial)?

675. Does God tempt anyone?

676. How is a person tempted?

677. Since wrath or man's anger does not produce the righteousness of God, what three things describe how we should act?

678. The knowledge of God's Word is important. What is more important?

679. Your religion is worthless if you don't do what?

680. What is the example the Bible uses to explain what pure religion is?

James: Chapter 2

681. What has God chosen the poor of this world to be rich in?

682. What happens to a person who keeps all the law but breaks one?

683. What is faith without action?

684. How is a believer able to show his faith?

685. In addition to people, who else believes there is one God?

686. How did Abraham demonstrate his faith?

James: Chapter 3

687. What does the tongue have the ability to do?

688. Where envy and selfish ambition exist, what else will be there?

689. Describe the wisdom that comes from above.

James: Chapter 4

690. Some do not have because they don't ask God for it. Yet why do others ask God and still not receive?

691. Those who try to be friends with this world make themselves an enemy of whom?

692. How do you get the devil to flee from you?

693. How do you get God to draw close to you?

694. When you humble yourself before the Lord, what will He do for you?

695. How does the Bible describe your life?

696. How does the book of James describe sin?

James: Chapter 5

697. If you're not supposed to swear an oath, what are you supposed to do?

698. If you are sick what does the Bible say to do?

699. When Elijah from the Old Testament prayed to stop the rain, how long was it before it rained again?

700. What will happen if you turn a sinner from the error of his ways?

First Peter: Chapter 1

701. What is more precious than gold?

702. What will you receive for your faith or trusting God?

703. If all flesh and the glory or beauty of man passes away, what endures forever?

First Peter: Chapter 2

704. Newborns desire milk. Why should a newborn Christian desire the spiritual milk of the Word?

705. Why should a Christian abstain from fleshly desires?

706. How should the liberty and freedom in Christ not be used?

First Peter: Chapter 3

707. What attribute found in ladies is so precious to God?

708. Since a husband and wife are equal partners in God's gift of life, what can hinder his prayers?

709. If the Lord turns His face against those who do evil, whose prayers are his ears open to?

710. What must a Christian always be ready to give a reason or a defense for?

First Peter: Chapter 4

711. Was the Gospel preached to the dead?

First Peter: Chapter 5

712. Why should you cast all your cares on God?

713. Who is the enemy of the Christian and what does he want to do to him?

Second Peter: Chapter 1

714. When adding knowledge to your faith, what two things come after increased knowledge or knowing God better?

715. Peter said he didn't make up fables or clever stories about the power of Christ. He was an eyewitness of what?

716. Why should you pay close attention to the prophecies of old?

717. If prophecies never came by the prophet, or the will of man, then how did they come?

Second Peter: Chapter 2

718. Why did God destroy the city of Sodom and Gomorrah?

Second Peter: Chapter 3

719. What will scoffers say in the last days?

720. How can you describe a day of the Lord in numbers?

721. Why is the Lord patient with mankind?

722. What will be the final fate of the heavens and the Earth on "the day of the Lord"?

723. What has God promised that people can look forward to after "the day of the Lord"?

First John: Chapter 1

724. The apostles recorded that which they saw with their own eyes, heard with their ears, and touched with their hands, so we might have what?

725. What does the word say about a person that says he has fellowship with God, yet he walks in darkness?

726. What happens if we walk in the light?

727. What are we doing if we say we have no sin?

728. What happens if we confess our sins?

729. What are we insinuating when we claim we have not sinned?

First John: Chapter 2

730. What advantage does Christ give a sinner?

731. If a person says he knows or follows Christ but does not keep His commandments, what can be said about that person?

732. We either love God or the things of the world. What are the things of the world that the Scriptures say we should not take part in?

733. What definition does the Bible give of a liar?

734. Who could be described as antichrist?

735. Is it possible to have the Father without the Son?

736. Why did John tell the readers that they didn't need a teacher?

First John: Chapter 3

737. What manner of love has the Father bestowed on us?

738. How does the Bible describe real love and how should we emulate it?

739. What can people expect from their prayers when they keep God's commandments and do what is pleasing to Him?

First John: Chapter 4

740. Why do the Scriptures indicate that when you belong to God you have overcome or already won the battle?

741. What happens when a person confesses Jesus as the Son of God?

742. What is God?

743. What does the Bible say about fear and love?

First John: Chapter 5

744. What condition must be met in order to have confidence that God hears your prayers?

745. The whole world is under the power of who?

746. Who is the true God and eternal life?

Second John: Chapter 1

747. If someone comes to your home and is not teaching the truth about Christ, what should you do?

Third John: Chapter 1

748. In what manner should Christians receive traveling teachers or missionaries of the faith?

Jude

749. Are there angels of Heaven that were disobedient to God?

750. How does John say we should "build ourselves up"?

We will now briefly return to the gospels, so turn back to the beginning of the New Testament. We will cover some key points found in Matthew, Mark, and Luke, before we conclude with the Book of the Revelation of Jesus Christ.

Chapters 1 and 2 of Matthew where covered in the beginning of the book. We will now move on to chapter 3.

Matthew: Chapter 3

751. What was John the Baptist preaching?

752. What was John the Baptist's clothing and food?

753. Where did the people come from to be baptized by John?

754. What did people do when they were baptized?

755. What did John call the Pharisees and Sadducees that came to the baptism place?

756. What did John say these leaders should do before being baptized?

757. Using an analogy of their day, what did John the Baptist say Christ would do with the wheat and the chaff after separating it?

Matthew: Chapter 4

758. Why was Jesus led by the Spirit into the desert?

759. How many days did He go without food?

760. When Jesus was hungry and tempted by the devil, what did Jesus say about bread?

761. When Jesus was tempted by satan to prove He was the Son of God by jumping off the top of the temple, what was His response?

762. What did the devil say he would give Jesus if He would worship him?

763. What was Jesus' response to the devil's offer?

764. Who ministered or cared for Christ after the devil left Him?

765. When Jesus started preaching, what was the first thing He said?

766. Who were the two brothers Jesus saw casting their nets into the sea?

767. What did Jesus say to the two fishermen?

768. What were the names of the two brothers mending their nets?

Matthew: Chapter 5

769. How are those that mourn blessed?

770. How are the meek going to be blessed?

771. How does God bless those who are persecuted for righteousness?

772. Why should you let your light or good deeds shine before men?

773. Concerning adultery, what else did Jesus say qualified as adultery?

774. In His example why did Jesus say it would be worth it to pluck out your own eye if it causes you to sin?

775. Giving examples, what did Jesus say you should do if someone slaps you on the cheek?

Matthew: Chapter 6

776. What did Jesus say happens if you do your charitable deeds to be seen by others?

777. What did Jesus say not to do when you pray; and what assurances do you have when you do pray?

778. What does the first verse of the Lord's prayer focus on?

779. After the Lord's prayer what did Jesus say happens if you refuse to forgive others?

780. What was the main reason Jesus gave to store your treasures in Heaven and not on Earth?

781. What did Jesus have to say about God and money?

782. Because our heavenly Father knows all our needs, what did Jesus say we should do first?

Matthew: Chapter 7

783. What did Jesus say about judging others?

784. According to Jesus if you ask, seek, or knock, what will happen?

785. Jesus said that many people refer to him as Lord, but if they don't do the will of the Father, what will He say to them?

786. What analogy did Jesus give about building on a solid foundation?

Matthew: Chapter 8

787. What impressed Jesus about the Roman Centurion who asked to have his servant healed?

788. Jesus cast out spirits with a word and healed the sick. How did the prophecy by Isaiah explain this?

789. While in a boat during a great storm, what did Jesus do that his disciples marveled at and what did they say in response?

Matthew: Chapter 9

790. After being questioned, why did Jesus say He ate with tax collectors and sinners?

791. The lady in need of a healing was satisfied just to touch the hem of Jesus' garment. What did Jesus say made her well?

792. When the two blind men cried out for mercy and healing, what question did Jesus ask them?

793. As Jesus taught and healed the multitudes he was moved to compassion. What was His concern?

Matthew: Chapter 10

794. What was the last name of Judas?

795. Jesus told His apostles, I am sending you out as sheep among wolves. How did he say they should act?

796. Why did Jesus say the apostles didn't need to worry about what to say in their defense if they were arrested?

797. If you are not to fear those that can kill the body, who did Jesus say you should fear?

798. What example did Jesus give to show that God watches everyone, every detail, and not one thing happens outside His will?

799. When we acknowledge Jesus before people or deny Him, what is His response?

Matthew: Chapter 11

800. When the disciples of John the Baptist asked Jesus if He was the Messiah or if they should look for another, what proof did Jesus offer?

801. Jesus said John the Baptist was the greatest of all people that had lived. Yet who did He say is even greater?

802. Jesus said His yoke is easy and His burden is light. What does He give to those who come to Him?

Matthew: Chapter 12

803. When they complained that Jesus was breaking the law, He recounted how King David broke the law in the temple. How did he relate himself to the holy temple?

804. What did Jesus do on the Sabbath that caused the Pharisees to call for His death?

805. Jesus said every sin of man can be forgiven except for which one?

806. Where do the words come from that a man speaks?

807. What did Jesus say would happen to every idle or careless word that a person speaks?

808. According to Jesus what will the words you speak do for you?

809. Did Jesus acknowledge the reality of Jonah and the whale?

810. What future event was Jesus describing through the story of Jonah and the whale?

811. Who did Jesus say were His mother, brother, and sisters?

Matthew: Chapter 13

812. Why did Jesus speak in parables?

813. There was a prophecy explaining why people wouldn't understand the parables of Jesus, what is the main theme of the prophecy?

814. What privilege did Jesus say the disciples had that many prophets and godly men did not have?

815. The seed was the Word of God. What did Jesus say was the meaning of the seed that fell by the wayside and was plucked by the birds?

816. What was meant by the seed that fell on stony places without much soil and immediately sprang up?

817. Some seeds fell among thorns, and the thorns sprang up and choked them. What is the meaning of this third part of the parable?

818. Some seeds fell on good soil and yielded a crop. What did Jesus say this means?

819. In another of Christ's parables, the servants wanted to gather up the tares or weeds that were planted among the good crop. Why did the owner say not to do it?

820. When Jesus explains the parable about the weeds, what does he say the field represents?

821. Who are the good seeds and who are the weeds?

822. Who is the enemy that planted the weeds?

823. What does the harvest represent?

824. Who will do the reaping of the harvest?

825. What will be the fate of the weeds in the field?

826. When the Son of man sends out His angels, what will they do?

827. What are the names of Jesus' four brothers?

828. Why did Jesus not do many miracles among the people of His hometown?

Matthew: Chapter 14

829. Who asked for John the Baptist's head on a platter?

830. What happened to the body of John the Baptist?

831. When Jesus walked to the boat on water did Peter then also walk on water?

832. When Jesus reached out His hand to save Peter from sinking what did He say to him?

Matthew: Chapter 15

833. Jesus was asked why His disciples disobeyed the traditions of the elders. What did Jesus say the traditions were actually doing?

834. Jesus quoted the prophecy of Isaiah. What does it point out about the commandments?

835. What did Jesus say defiles a man?

Matthew: Chapter 16

836. What was Peter's answer when Christ asked him, "Who do you say that I am?"

837. What did Peter say when Jesus told him about the events concerning His death and resurrection?

838. When Peter took Christ aside and corrected Him, what did Christ say?

839. What does Jesus say is more important than anything you gain from this world?

Matthew: Chapter 17

840. When Jesus took Peter, James, and John up on a high mountain, what happened to Jesus?

841. Who appeared and talked to Jesus in the presence of Peter, James, and John?

842. A voice came from a bright cloud that overshadowed them. What did the voice say?

843. The disciples were disappointed that they couldn't cure a man's son. What was the reason Jesus gave for their lack of success?

844. Where did Peter get the money to pay the temple tax for himself and Jesus?

Matthew: Chapter 18

845. What example did Jesus use to show how serious it was when you cause a child to sin?

846. Did Jesus indicate that a child has an angel in Heaven?

847. What happens when two or three people are gathered together in the name of Jesus?

Matthew: Chapter 19

848. What does Jesus say happens to a man and a woman who are joined in marriage?

849. When a rich young man asked Jesus about eternal life, what caused the man to leave in a saddened condition?

850. How hard did Christ say it is for a rich man to enter Heaven?

851. When the disciples were concerned about how anyone would make it to Heaven, what did Christ tell them?

852. What did Christ say about the first and the last in Heaven?

Matthew: Chapter 20

853. Jesus said He didn't come to be served but to do what?

Matthew: Chapter 21

854. When Jesus sent His disciples out for a donkey and a colt, what prophecy did this help fulfill?

Matthew: Chapter 22

855. When asked is it lawful to pay tax money to Caesar, what did Jesus say?

856. What did Jesus tell the Sadducees about marriage in Heaven and what the dead would be like?

857. What was the quote Jesus used from God to prove to the Sadducees that those who die are still alive?

858. When asked a question by the Pharisees, what two things did Jesus say summed up all the law?

Matthew: Chapter 23

859. Jesus told the people to follow the rules set up for them by the Scribe and Pharisee leaders, but what didn't He want the people to do?

860. Jesus criticized the Scribes (teachers of the law) and Pharisees for many things. One criticism was that they tried to look righteous on the outside, while on the inside they were really just what?

861. What endearing way did Jesus refer to the children of Jerusalem and what did He long to do for them?

862. Jesus quoted Psalms from the Old Testament when He told the people they wouldn't see him again until they say what?

Matthew: Chapter 24

863. When Jesus disciples were showing Him the buildings of the temple what did Jesus prophecy or predict would happen to the buildings?

864. Sitting on the Mount of Olives what two questions did the disciples ask Jesus?

865. Did Jesus say there would be false Christs in the future?

866. What did Christ say about the good news or the gospel concerning the end of the age?

867. After the tribulation of the days Christ described, what will happen to the sun, moon, stars and heavens?

868. How will the Son of Man return?

869. Following the return of Christ what will the angels do after the sound of the trumpet?

870. Jesus says Heaven and Earth will pass away, but what will remain forever?

871. Who knows exactly the day and the hour when Heaven and Earth will pass away?

872. Does Christ acknowledge the existence of Noah?

873. Did the people in the day of Noah have any idea that a flood was about to take place?

874. According to Christ will people have any idea that He is about to return?

875. Jesus says since He will be returning at any hour, what should you do?

Matthew: Chapter 25

876. Concerning the 10 virgins, who was allowed to attend the wedding?

877. After the unprepared virgins returned and said, "Lord, Lord open the door," what did the Bridegroom say to them?

878. When the Son of Man sits on the throne and all the nations are gathered before Him, how will He separate them?

879. What did Jesus say the people that are inheriting His Kingdom did for Him while on Earth?

880. What did Christ say was the fate of those separated to His left, the goats?

Matthew: Chapter 26

881. When Jesus was praying in the garden of Gethsemane, what did He ask the Father to do for Him?

882. Was Jesus willing to submit to the Father's will?

Matthew: Chapter 27

883. What did Judas say when he returned the 30 pieces of silver?

884. Who were those mocking Christ when He was on the cross?

885. While Jesus was on the cross when was there darkness over all the land?

886. At the ninth hour, or 3 p.m., what did Jesus say?

887. What happened to the veil of the temple when Jesus gave up His Spirit?

888. When the Earth quaked and the rocks were split, what happened to some of the bodies of believers?

889. What concerns did the chief priests and Pharisees go to Pilate about?

890. After Pilate gave a guard to the Jewish leaders what did they do?

Mark: Chapter 1

891. What happened to the stone in front of the tomb's entrance?

892. How did the guards react when they saw the angel?

893. What did the angel tell the ladies at the tomb?

894. As the women rushed to tell the disciples their discovery, who did they meet on the way?

895. When the Jewish leaders gave money to the soldiers what did they tell them to say?

896. When Jesus met the disciples on the mountain what did He say to them?

Mark: Chapter 1

897. The man with the evil spirit recognized Jesus as the Holy One of God. What was the man concerned about?

Mark: Chapter 2

898. What was Jesus proving to the scribes (teachers of the law) when He healed the paralytic?

Mark: Chapter 3

899. When Jesus appointed 12 apostles, what did He give them before sending them out to preach?

900. Where did the teachers of the law say Jesus got His power to cast out demons?

901. How did Jesus explain that it was impossible for Him to receive His power from Satan?

Mark: Chapter 4

902. Jesus related the Kingdom of God to a mustard seed. What is unique about a mustard seed?

Mark: Chapter 5

903. When Jesus called out the evil spirit from the man that lived in the tombs, what did the spirit say his name was and why?

904. When the man who was demon possessed asked Jesus if he could stay with Him, what did Jesus tell him to do?

Mark: Chapter 6

905. When Jesus came to His own country to teach why were the people amazed at His wisdom?

Mark: Chapter 8

906. While in Dalmanutha the Pharisees disputed with Jesus. What caused Him to give out a deep sigh?

907. "What did Jesus say would happen if we are ashamed of Him and His words?"

Mark: Chapter 9

908. When a man brought his convulsing son to Christ for healing, what did Christ tell him?

909. What was the Father's response to Jesus?

910. What did the disciples argue about on the road to Capernaum?

911. What did Jesus tell the disciples to set them straight about their desire for an elevated position?

Mark: Chapter 10

912. When the Pharisees quoted Moses about a man having permission to divorce his wife, why did Jesus say this permission was given?

913. When the parents brought their children to see Jesus, what did the disciples do that displeased Him?

914. What happens if a person does not have the faith of a child or receive the Kingdom of God as a little child?

915. What did Jesus say to encourage those who had to leave family or homes for His sake?

Mark: Chapter 11

916. When Jesus went to the fig tree but found no fruit, what did He say?

917. The next morning when they passed by the fig tree, what was its condition?

918. Why wouldn't the Pharisees answer Jesus when He asked them if the baptism of John was from Heaven or from men?

Mark: Chapter 12

919. What did the owner of the vineyard do as a last resort to receive the harvest of fruit that was rightfully his?

920. What did the workers do with the son of the owner of the vineyards, and why?

921. What did Jesus say the owner of the vineyard would do to the tenants after they had killed his son?

922. At the conclusion of the story of the vineyard, what was the quotation given by Christ to help complete his lesson?

923. What did the Pharisees realize after Jesus had given this illustration?

Mark: Chapter 13

924. According to the parable of the fig tree when do you know summer is near?

Mark: Chapter 14

925. For the Passover meal how did the two disciples know where to go?

926. Quote the Scripture from Zechariah that Jesus used to describe His disciples deserting Him.

Mark: Chapter 15

927. What was Barabbas in prison for?

928. How did the soldiers mock Christ?

Mark: Chapter 16

929. When did the ladies go to the tomb to anoint the body of Christ?

930. What concerned the ladies as they went to the tomb?

931. What day did Jesus rise from the dead?

Luke was covered in the beginning of this book up to Chapter 3, verse 23. We will now complete the rest of the story from there.

Luke: Chapter 3

932. Jewish genealogy allows them to trace their ancestors all the way back to who?

933. Was Noah a descendant of Methuselah?

Luke: Chapter 4

934. In the synagogue Jesus read from the prophet Isaiah. What did He say to everyone watching Him?

Luke: Chapter 5

935. What astonished Peter that caused him to ask Jesus to depart from him because he was a sinful man?

936. After Jesus healed the leper, what did He tell him to do?

937. Men brought a paralyzed man to Jesus for healing. What did they do that showed how determined they were to help him?

Luke: Chapter 6

938. What did Jesus say about giving?

Luke: Chapter 7

939. Why did Jesus have compassion for the widow in the city of Nain?

Luke: Chapter 8

940. How many evil spirits was Mary Magdalene delivered from?

Luke: Chapter 9

941. When Jesus sent out his disciples to preach what did He tell them to take with them?

942. Pertaining to the Kingdom of God, once you put your hand to the plow what should you do?

Luke: Chapter 10

943. When the disciples returned full of joy because the spirits obeyed them, what did Jesus say they should really rejoice about?

944. What did the (good) Samaritan do for the wounded man that the priest did not do?

945. While Mary was sitting at the feet of Jesus listening to His teachings, what was her sister Martha doing?

946. Mary wasn't helping Martha. Why did Jesus defend her?

Luke: Chapter 11

947. A woman from the crowd said God bless your mother and the womb that you came from. Who did Jesus say was even more blessed?

948. What did Jesus say was the lamp of the body?

Luke: Chapter 12

949. What did Jesus say would be shouted from the rooftops?

950. What did Jesus say about the person who adds to his possessions daily and is content in them?

Luke: Chapter 13

951. Who did Jesus say was responsible for the condition of the lady who had been doubled over for 18 years?

952. How did the Lord compare the mustard seed to the Kingdom of Heaven?

953. The question was asked of Jesus, "Lord, are only a few people going to be saved?" What was His answer?

Luke: Chapter 14

954. What blessing will you receive when you entertain those who cannot repay you?

Luke: Chapter 15

955. Using a parable, how did Jesus describe God's concern for each and every lost soul?

956. What do the angels in Heaven do when a sinner repents?

957. In the story of the prodigal son, which of the two sons wanted his inheritance immediately?

958. When the prodigal son ran out of money, what job was he willing to take and what food was he willing to eat?

959. When the prodigal son came home to his father, what was the attitude of the son?

960. What was the father's attitude towards his returning son?

961. What was the attitude of the older brother when his younger sibling returned?

Luke: Chapter 16

962. In the parable about the rich man, what did Jesus say happened to Lazarus when he died?

963. Where did the rich man end up when he died?

964. When the rich man saw Lazarus with Father Abraham, what did he ask Abraham to do for him and why?

965. Was the rich man allowed to cross over to Lazarus or vice versa?

966. Why did the rich man beg Abraham to send Lazarus to his family?

967. Abraham said the rich man's family already had knowledge of something. What was it that Abraham said they "have" and what should they do about it?

968. What did the rich man think would happen if someone could return to his family from the dead?

969. What was Abraham's reply to the rich man's request to send someone from the dead to his family?

Luke: Chapter 17

970. Jesus healed 10 men of leprosy. How many returned to thank him?

Luke: Chapter 18

971. Why did Jesus tell the parable about the persistent widow?

972. What did Jesus have to say about the self-righteous man who prayed at the temple and the one who admitted the fact that he was a sinner?

Luke: Chapter 19

973. In the story about the 10 servants, what will happen to those who use well what they are given?

Luke: Chapter 20

974. Did Jesus acknowledge the fact that Moses wrote about the burning bush?

Luke: Chapter 21

975. Why was Jesus so impressed with the widow and her gift of two pennies?

Luke: Chapter 22

976. At the last Passover meal for Jesus what did He say about wine?

977. When Jesus was praying in the garden what was a physical result of His agonizing prayer?

Luke: Chapter 23

978. When they crucified Christ, what did He pray *for* the people that were doing this to Him?

979. Who was the first person to be in Paradise with Jesus after He died?

Luke: Chapter 24

980. When Jesus appeared and walked with Cleopas and another man, what did they question Him about?

981. As Jesus walked with the two men what was He explaining to them?

982. What happened to these two men, and then Jesus, after Jesus blessed the bread and gave it to them?

983. When the men rose up and found the eleven others, what was the first thing they said to them?

984. While eating in the presence of the disciples where did Jesus say the words were written that were about Him?

985. After telling the disciples about the words written concerning Him, what did Jesus do for the disciples?

986. What was the last thing Jesus did after blessing the disciples?

We will only touch on the first and last chapters of the Book of the Revelation because it requires in-depth study and interpretation in order to fully understand its meaning. It is a very interesting book, full of visions about future events. For a deeper study on the Book of the Revelation we suggest you find a good Bible teaching church or use one of the many study books written on the subject.

The Book of the Revelation: Chapter 1

987. Who was the revelation about?

988. Who is blessed through the Book of the Revelation?

989. Who wrote this letter of revelation and who was it sent to?

990. How did John describe Jesus Christ?

991. When Christ is coming in the clouds, who will see Him?

992. When Jesus returns what will all the nations of the Earth do?

993. Where was John when he heard a loud voice like a trumpet?

994. What did the loud voice tell John to do?

995. When John turned to see the voice that spoke to him, who did he see in the midst of the seven lampstands?

996. After reassuring John not to be afraid, how did He describe himself?

997. What did the Son of Man ask John to write about?

The Book of the Revelation: Chapter 22

998. How does the Lord Jesus describe himself?

999. What is given for free to those that thirst?

1000. At the end of the Book of the Revelation, when does Jesus Christ say He is coming?

1001. What do you think the final question should be, and do you know the answer?